1. Brush powdered makeup blush or soft pastel chalk on the cheeks. For more life, blush forehead, tips of nose and chin. If using soft pastels, add a small amount of gray under the eyes.

2. Color inside eye area with a White gel pen or White acrylic paint. Allow each coat to dry. Line top and bottom lids with Brown. Add a circle of Black in each eye. When dry, add a circle of Light Blue filling Black circle almost completely leaving thin rim around the Light Blue to make eye more visible. Add a smaller Black circle in the center of each eye for the pupil. Highlight the top of the pupil with a tiny speck of White. A dot of Red can be added at inside corner of eyes near the bridge of the nose.

3. Use a Red gel pen or acrylic paints to color the lips. Line the outside edges with a darker shade of Red.

4. Spray head with matte acrylic spray sealer to preserve pen, chalk or paint.

5. Cut lengths of curly hair. Apply at base of neck with Fabri-Tac. Work up toward crown of head. Style hair when the glue is completely dry.

Add a little 'Bee Happy' face and big feet with polished toenails to a flowerpot. Fill the flowerpot with bright paper shreds and sunny flowers for a perky presentation!

Perky Pot

MATERIALS: Sculpey whimsical dolls flexible push mold • Block of Beige Premo clay • Block of Terra Cotta Sculpey III clay • Liquid Sculpey • 4" terra cotta flowerpot • *Stampendous* rubber stamps ('Bee Happy', bee, small flower) • Ink pads (Black, Green, Red) • Curly doll hair • Scrap of Yellow fringe • Small silk flower with leaves • Silk flowers • Green paper shreds • Fabri-Tac • Acrylic paints • Gel pens

INSTRUCTIONS: Roll out a thin sheet of Terra Cotta. Stamp 'Bee Happy' and 4 flowers, cut out curved shape. Stamp a line of small flowers and cut a 1/2" x 8" strip. Attach shape to front of flowerpot and strip to rim leaving room for face. Bake flowerpot at 275°F for 30 minutes. Push balls of Beige into face #1, ears and feet and place mold in freezer for 90 seconds. Pop out pieces. Attach ears to face. Coat back of face and top of feet with Liquid Sculpey. Position face on rim of pot and feet on bottom. Roll small ball of clay and attach to bottom back so flowerpot will stand, bake flowerpot. Let cool. Color face with acrylic paints or gel pens. Glue curly hair, flower and leaf on head and fringe under chin. Stamp bees around flowerpot. Fill flowerpot with flowers and paper shreds.

1. Roll a sheet of clay using a pasta machine.

2. Cut a strip of clay for rim of the flowerpot.

3. Cut sign from clay and rubber stamp.

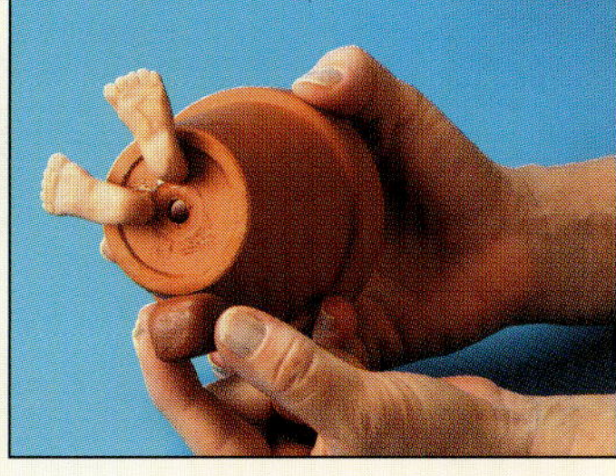

4. Press a ball of clay on bottom of the flower pot so it will stand.

Tooth Fairy Tin

1. Roll a sheet of clay using a pasta machine.

2. Place the tin on the clay and trim clay to size.

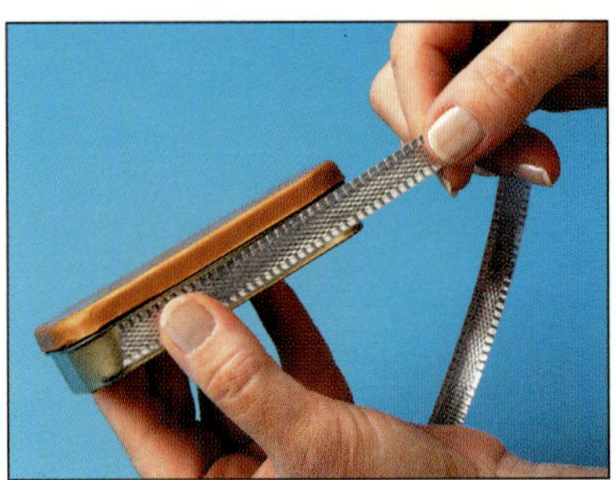

3. Trim clay from around the lid with a clay blade. Bake.

4. Glue the ribbon around the box bottom.

5. Press the sign and doll head on the lid.

MATERIALS: Sculpey grandma/grandpa flexible push mold • Premo clay (block of Beige, block of Gold, ½ block of Copper, ¼ block of Bronze, ⅛ block of Translucent) • Liquid Sculpey • Altoid tin • 'Surprise Inside' rubber stamp • Black ink pad • 8" of 1" White lace • 6" of ⅛" Gold ribbon • 12" of ½" Gold mesh ribbon • Gray curly doll hair • 1" of Gold star garland • 1" of 2mm Gold strung pearls • Fabri-Tac • Acrylic paints • Gel pens • Black fine tip pen

INSTRUCTIONS: Coat lid of an empty, clean Altoid tin with Liquid Sculpey. Roll out 3" x 5" sheet of Gold clay and place on top of tin. Press smoothly into place. Trim off excess around edges. Bake at 275°F for 30 minutes.

Roll a 2" square of Copper clay. Stamp and cut out curved shape. Roll a 1" square of Translucent clay and cut a triangle. Bake pieces.

Push balls of Beige into face and ear molds. Freeze mold for 90 seconds and pop out pieces. Coat back of face, ears and Copper stamped piece with Liquid Sculpey. Position pieces on lid. Roll a Bronze snake, press around edges of Copper piece and bake tin. Let cool. Color facial features with acrylic paints or gel pens. Using Fabri-Tac, attach hair and star garland to head and 2 pearls to each ear. Gather and attach lace under chin. Tie ⅛" ribbon bow and glue on lace. Write 'Tooth Fairy' on triangle with Black pen and glue under bow. Glue ½" ribbon around bottom of tin.

Purple Tin

MATERIALS: Sculpey flexible face and Etruscan push molds • Blocks of Beige Premo clay • Sculpey III clay (Purple, Lavender, Silver, Violet) • SuperFlex clay (Beige, Yellow) • Liquid Sculpey • Pink flower cane • 5" round tin • Rubber stamps ('Surprise Inside', tiny flower) • Ink pads (Black, Silver, Gold) • Lavender cardstock • Two Lavender ribbon flowers with pearl centers • Needle tool • Fabri-Tac • Acrylic paints • Gel pens

INSTRUCTIONS: Cover lid of tin with Liquid Sculpey. Roll a sheet of Purple, press on lid and trim. Bake at 275°F for 30 minutes. Blend Violet and Silver clay.

Mold face following instructions. Roll extremely thin logs of Yellow and Beige SuperFlex and coil around needle tool. Cut desired lengths and bake on tool. Carefully remove and attach to face with Liquid Sculpey. Bake face. Paint face.

Mold 4 Etruscan pieces. Shape over lid of tin, remove and bake. Cut curved shape from a sheet of Lavender clay, stamp message and bake. Roll cane to desired size, cut out flowers and bake. Stamp Lavender cardstock with Gold and Silver flowers. Cut a 4" circle and a ½" strip. Glue circle in center of lid and strip around rim. Remove pearls from one ribbon flower and glue it behind face. Use 2 pearls for earrings. Glue other flower on head and head on tin. Glue remaining clay pieces referring to the photo.

Terrific Tin Boxes

Small tins covered with clay are as much fun to receive as the surprise inside, and the tins are sure to be 'keepers'!

- *Roll out the clay.*
- *Cover the tin and trim clay.*
- *Mold doll head.*
- *Make trim.*
- *Make sign.*
- *Assemble and you are finished!*

1. Rubber stamp the clay sheet with daisies.

2. Cut out the frame and the frame center.

3. Fold the molded hands around the sign.

4. Glue the molded items and signs in place.

Friendship Frame Magnet

Give your best friend a gift that says how much you appreciate her. Personalize the faces by matching hair colors, eyes and makeup styles.

MATERIALS: Sculpey miniature dolls flexible push mold • Premo clay (block of Beige, 2 blocks of White, pinch of Cobalt Blue, pinch of Cadium Yellow) • Liquid Sculpey • Rubber stamps (*Hampton Art Stamps* daisies frame, 'True Friends Always') • Ink pads (Black, Yellow) • Two colors of curly doll hair • 2 small round magnets • Fabri-Tac • Acrylic paints • Gels pens

INSTRUCTIONS: Combine block of White with a pinch of Cobalt Blue and blend to make Light Blue. Roll out Light Blue clay and stamp with Yellow daisies frame. Cut out center of frame. Roll out a Light Blue sheet and stamp message with Black ink. Cut around message. Combine a block of White and a pinch of Cadium Yellow, roll out and cut frame backing. Coat back of frame with Liquid Sculpey, place on Yellow backing piece and bake at 275°F for 30 minutes. Push balls of Beige into faces #2 and #3 and hands #3. Place mold in freezer for 90 seconds. Pop out pieces. Using Liquid Sculpey, position faces, hands and message on frame and bake. When cool, color facial features with acrylic paints or gel pens. Glue curly hair on heads with Fabri-Tac. Color flowers on frame with gel pens. Glue magnets on back of frame.

Birthday Photo Album

Collect all your photos from a memorable birthday celebration and display them in an album with unusual clay covers.

MATERIALS: Sculpey angelic/young adult face flexible push mold • Premo clay (2 blocks of Turquoise, 4 blocks of White, block of Fuchsia, block of Beige) • Liquid Sculpey • Rubber stamps ('Happy Birthday', 'You Take the Cake', small swirl) • Ink pads (Blue, Pink) • Photo insert book for 4" x 6" photos • Black curly doll hair • 1½ yards of Purple rattail cord • Pink tulle • Skewer • Fabri-Tac • Acrylic paint • Gel pens

INSTRUCTIONS: Combine 1½ blocks of Turquoise with 3 blocks of White and blend to make Light Turquoise. Roll out two 5" x 7" sheets. Stamp swirl background on sheets with Blue and Pink ink. Use a skewer to make holes for lacing book. Remember to flip back cover over and align sheets as you make holes. Bake sheets at 275°F for 30 minutes.

Combine one block of White with a pinch of Fuchsia and blend to make Light Pink. Roll a sheet of Light Pink and stamp words. Cut out words and bake. Let cool. Use Liquid Sculpey as an adhesive to attach Fuchsia border around the baked words. Texture the border with swirl stamp. Bake.

Push balls of conditioned Beige into face #3, ears and hand molds. Place in the freezer for 90 seconds and pop out pieces. Coat backs of stamped words, face, ears and hands with Liquid Sculpey. Position pieces on front sheet. Allow room for an outer border. Bake. Attach a Turquoise border around cool 5" x 7" sheets using Liquid Sculpey. Texture border with swirls and bake. Color the facial features with acrylic paints or gel pens. Glue curly hair on head. Cut 4" of tulle, knot in the center and glue on hair. Cut two 6" pieces of tulle, roll into tubes, fold in half and glue in place for arms. Glue front and back of photo book to 5" x 7" covers using Fabri-Tac. Let dry thoroughly.

Insert cord in bottom hole of front cover. Pull through hole on back cover until half of cord length is on front side and other half is on back. Starting with front piece of cord, thread through next hole up on front cover, and pull out through next hole on back. Continue to work up spine of book with same length of cord going through each hole. When you reach the top, return to bottom and lace other half of cord through each hole to the top. Tie loosely at top allowing room to add photos to book. Tighten cord as needed. Fill album with pictures.

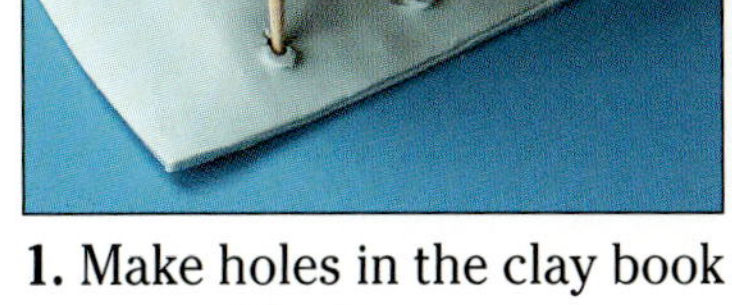

1. Make holes in the clay book covers with skewer.

2. Rubber stamp design on the book cover.

3. Use Liquid Sculpy and press border around words.

4. Lace the covers together with cord.

Baskets for Goodies

Fill the bellies of these baskets with goodies and use them for centerpieces. Coordinate the fabric to the party theme.

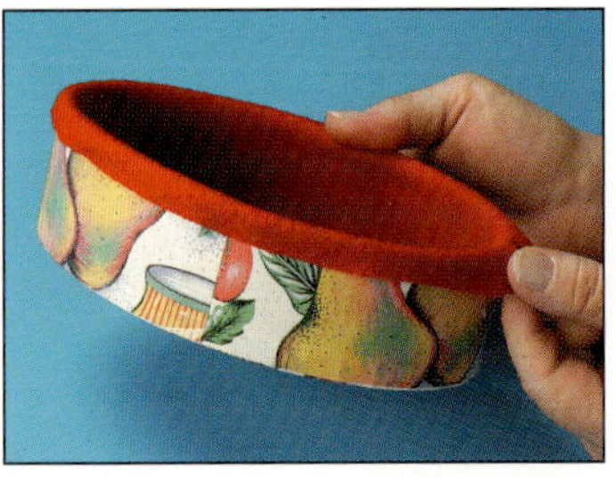

1. Roll the felt or fabric over top of edge of the box and glue in place.

2. Glue the arms, legs and head in place.

3. Thread elastic through the casing in fabric.

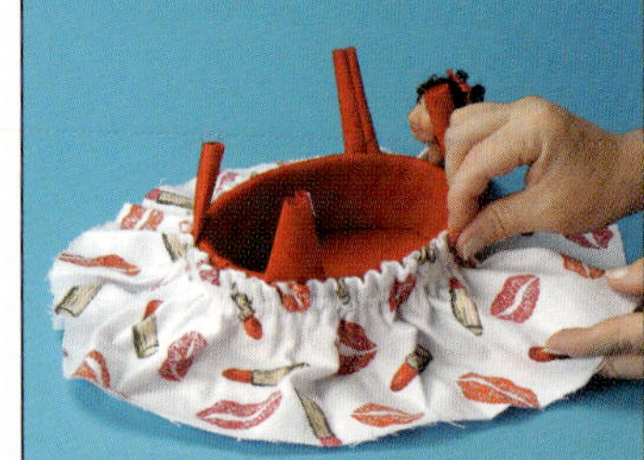

4. Place fabric around top of box, pull tight and tie a knot in elastic.

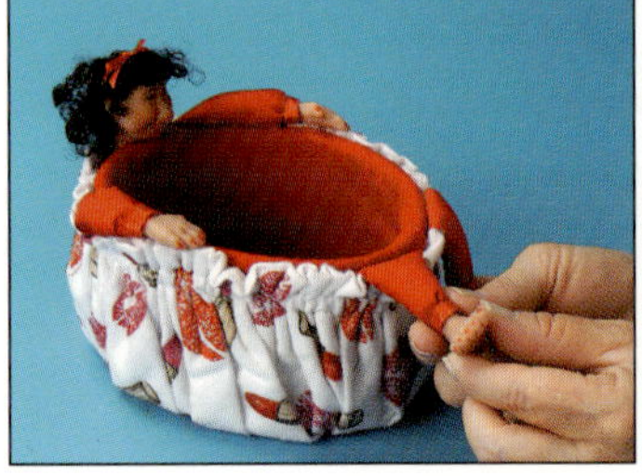

5. Hot glue the feet and hands in place.

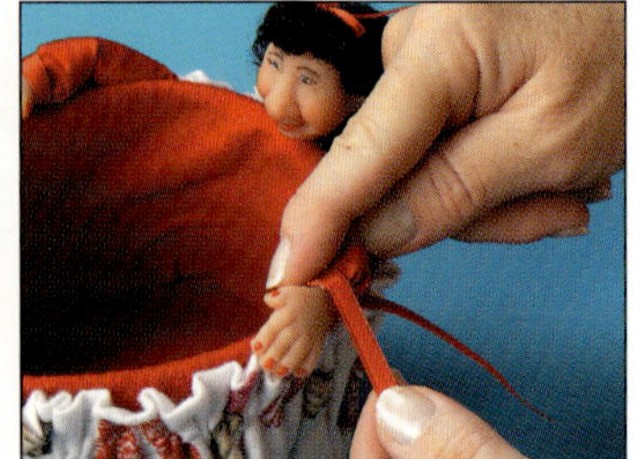

6. Hot glue ribbon around the hands.

Lips Basket

MATERIALS: Finished doll head • 4½" x 5½" x 3" papier-mâché box • Red felt • Lip print fabric • 8" of ⅛" and 10" of ¼" Red satin ribbon • 6" of ⅝" Red sheer ribbon • Black curly doll hair

INSTRUCTIONS: Make basket following instructions. Glue ¼" ribbon around wrists. Tie with ⅛" ribbon bow and glue on hair. Wrap ⅝" ribbon around neck and tie knot.

Scarecrow Basket

MATERIALS: Finished doll head • 3½" x 4½" x 2½" papier-mâché box • Brown and squares print fabric • Beige felt • 2½" burlap hat • Raffia

INSTRUCTIONS: Make basket following instructions. Insert raffia at wrists and ankles. Glue fabric around wrists and ankles and tie fabric strip around neck. Glue raffia hair and hat on head.

Basket Instructions

MATERIALS: Sculpey character flexible face mold • 1½ blocks of Beige Premo clay • Oval or round papier-mâché box • Polyester fiberfill • Choice of fabric • Felt • Yard of thin elastic • Tapestry needle • Tape • Fabri-Tac • Acrylic paint • Gel pens • Hot glue

INSTRUCTIONS: Select a theme for basket and choose fabric. Follow instructions for molding and bringing to life a character face and head. Mold feet and hands, extending the mold at the ankle and wrist areas. To cover inside of box, drape fabric inside, rough fit fabric or felt with edges extending over sides, or measure inside of box and cut fabric or felt to fit exactly. Glue in place.

To cover outside of box, measure circumference of box. Cut a strip of fabric long enough to go around outside of box twice. Width should be 3" more than height of box. Fold over top edge of fabric 1½" and press down. Sew 2 parallel seams the length of fabric to make a casing for elastic. Thread a tapestry needle with elastic and thread through casing. Make sure to leave elastic at each end.

Hot glue head on box. Use tape to reinforce position of head. Let dry. Fit outside fabric around box. Pull elastic cord tight and knot. Even out fabric so it looks like ruffles.

Cut out fabric doll leg and arm patterns. Sew leg and arm pieces folded with right sides together and turn right side out. Place legs and arms under outside fabric and check for proper position. Hand stitch arms and legs to outside fabric. Edges of pieces will remain tucked under fabric. Place a small amount of fiberfill in each leg and arm to give shape. Place feet and hands inside tubes. Make sure thumbs are closest to inside of basket. Secure feet and hands by sewing a running stitch around ankle and wrist areas, pull thread tight and knot. Finish arms and legs by covering edges of fabric at wrists and ankles with strips of folded fabric or pieces of ribbon. Run a line of Fabri-Tac around edges of the box to secure ruffles.

Glue hands in place. Cover neckline with ribbon, fabric or lace. Glue bottom edge of ruffles on bottom of box. Cover box bottom with felt. Fill basket with small gifts, bath oil beads, soaps, candy or other snacks.

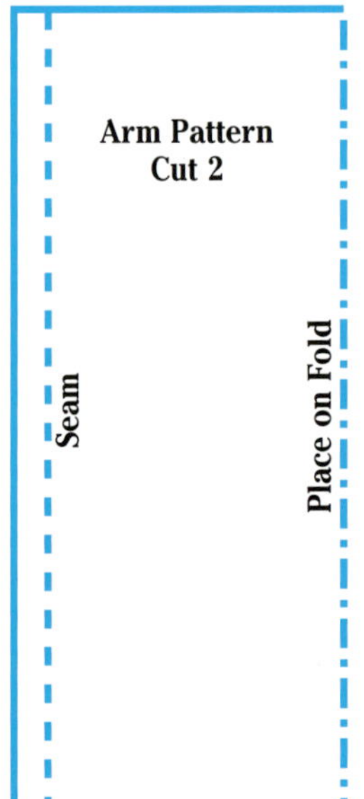

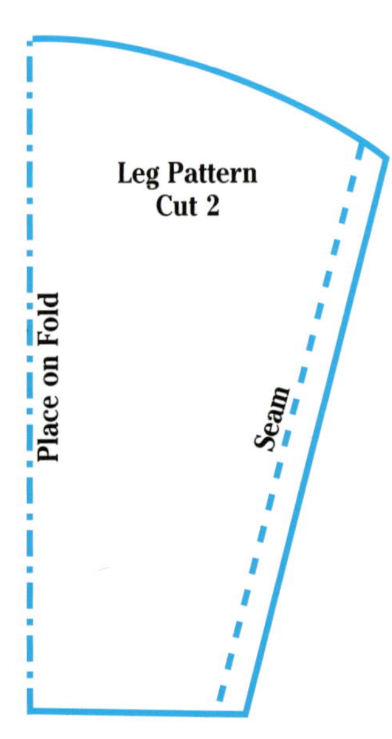

Angel

MATERIALS: Finished doll head • White star print fabric • 3" sheer White angel wings • 6" and 18" pieces of ⅝" White lace • 3" of Gold star garland • 8" of ¼" White satin ribbon • 12" of ¼" Pink satin ribbon • 6" of ⅛" Gold ribbon • White flower stamens • Red curly doll hair
INSTRUCTIONS: Make doll following instructions. Glue White ribbon around wrists and ankles. Gather 18" of lace around neck and secure. Tie Gold ribbon bow, glue in place. Glue angel wings on back. Make halo with garland and glue on head. Cut Pink ribbon in half and wrap each piece near the top of a single stamen, glue ends. Bundle stamens and gather 6" of lace around bundle. Glue bundle on front of body and hands in place.

Stuffed Doll Instructions

MATERIALS: Sculpey flexible character face mold • 1½ blocks of Beige Premo clay • ¼ yard of fabric • Polyester fiberfill • Beanbag fill • Needle and thread • Curly doll hair • Ribbon, bias tape or lace • Fabri-Tac

INSTRUCTIONS: Following instructions, mold hands and feet. Extend wrist and ankle areas of hands and feet by adding small amounts of clay to molded piece. Give character to doll by following the instructions for bringing face to life. Add hair.

Cut 2 each of body, arm and leg pieces from fabric. Fold each arm and leg piece in half with right sides together. Stitch side seam and turn right side out. Place one body semicircle right side up with straight edge at top. Place 2 leg pieces in center of body fabric with wide end of leg matching straight edge of body. Place arm pieces on far sides of legs matching tops to straight edge of body. Carefully place other body semicircle wrong side up over other pieces matching edges.

Sew a straight seam across top edge of all pieces. Make sure to catch all arm and leg pieces in seam. Unfold. You should have a circle of fabric with leg and arm pieces sewn in center. Double-thread needle and run gathering stitch around outside arc of circle. Pull tight to form body with top opening for doll head. Pour a tablespoon or more of bean bag fill into body to give added weight. Stuff body with fiberfill. Insert completed doll head in opening, pull stitches tight and secure ends of thread.

Stuff arms and legs with fiberfill. Gather ends of arms, insert hands, pull thread tight and secure. Repeat for legs. Glue bias tape or ribbon around wrists for a finished look. Add lace or ribbon around neckline to hide stitching.

Body Pattern - Cut 2

Arm & Leg Patterns on Page 8.

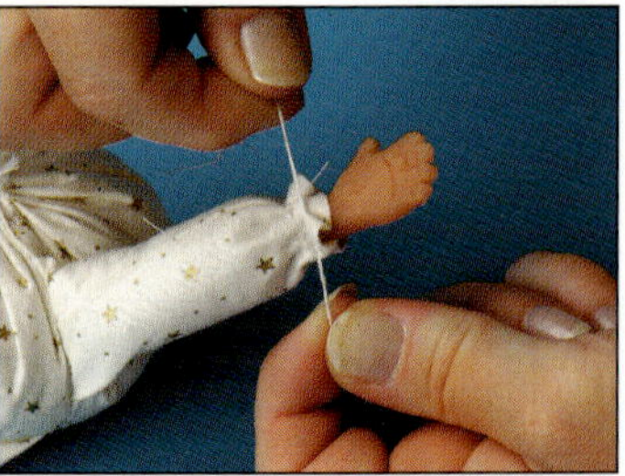

1. Sew arms and legs and turn right side out.

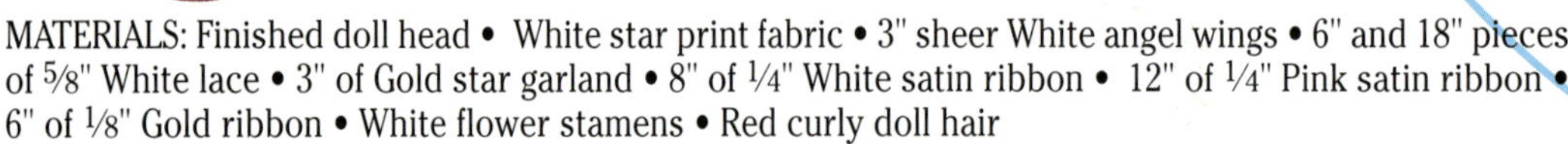

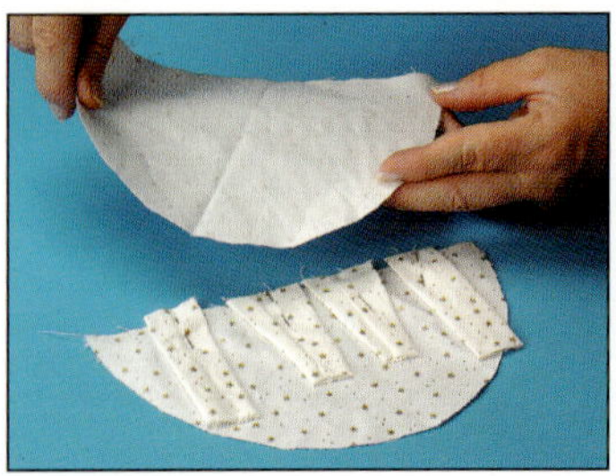

2. Sandwich arms and legs between body pieces.

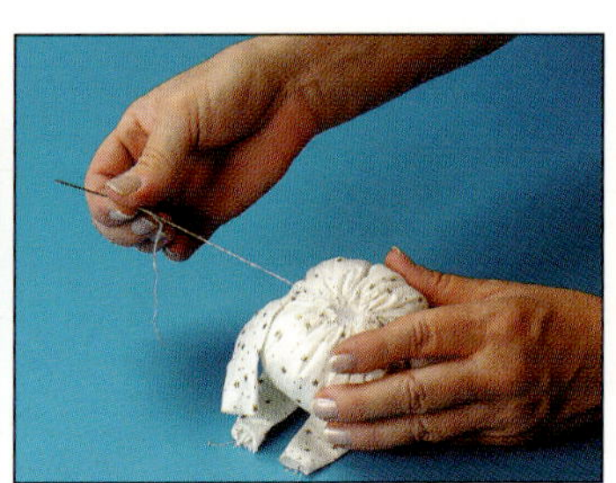

3. Stuff the body and gather the neck.

4. Stuff the arms and legs.

5. Place feet and hands in openings, gather fabric and tie to secure.

Santa Claus

MATERIALS: Finished doll head • Red stripe fabric • White felt • 10mm Red jingle bell • Gold wire • White curly doll hair • Round-nose pliers

INSTRUCTIONS: Make doll following instructions. Make glasses. Glue glasses on head and beard and mustache on face. Make hat using pattern. Sew jingle bell on tip. Glue on head. Glue strips of felt around bottom of hat, wrists and ankles.

Mrs. Claus

MATERIALS: Finished doll head • Plaid fabric • White felt • 12" of ⁵⁄₈" White lace • Red wire • Miniature reindeer • White curly doll hair • Round-nose pliers

INSTRUCTIONS: Make doll following instructions. Glue strips of felt around wrists and ankles. Make glasses and glue on head. Gather 12" of lace around neck and secure. Glue reindeer on body and hands on reindeer.

Wonderful Stuffed Dolls

Stuff plump little dolls and use them on Christmas trees or as wreath decorations. They can be dressed to match a holiday theme, a wedding, a shower or a birthday. Let your imagination fly!

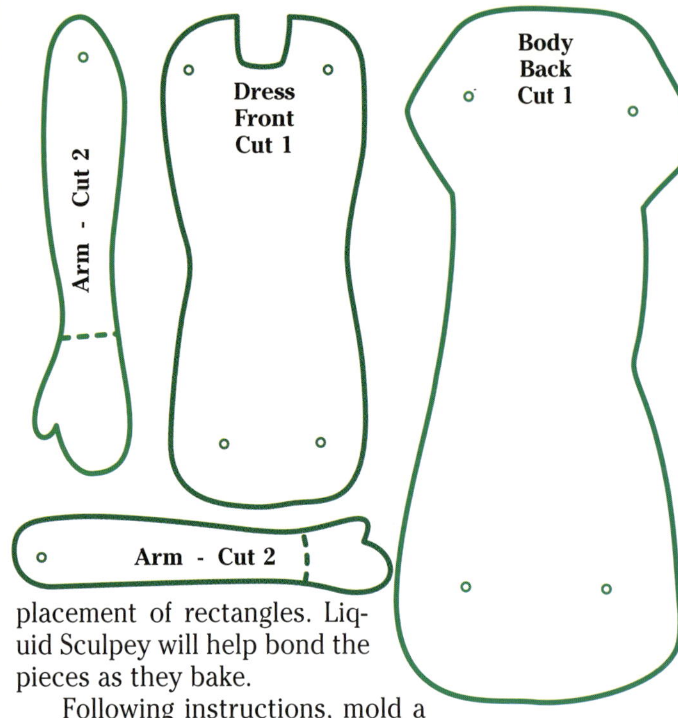

placement of rectangles. Liquid Sculpey will help bond the pieces as they bake.

Following instructions, mold a face. Place a small amount of Liquid Sculpey along neckline on back piece. This is where the head will be attached and it is important to make a strong bond. Attach head by adding some clay to face for neck. Add and smooth together additional clay at neckline. For more strength, add more clay to back of head and back of neckline and smooth. Dip eye pin into Liquid Sculpey, press it through top of head and secure on dress below neck. Bake the back piece and head. Make a ½" multicolor clay bead with a large hole and bake.

Cut 2 leg pieces from sheet of skin tone clay rolled through pasta machine at #1 setting. If you want dimensional feet, cut off legs at ankle as indicated by dotted lines on leg pattern. Mold 2 larger size feet. Make small slits in tops of molded feet. Attach legs to feet by inserting in slit and smoothing ankle area. Use a needle tool to make hole in the thighs as indicated on pattern. Repeat for the arms. Add thin clay ropes for bracelets. Bake the arms and legs.

To assemble, thread 8" pieces of floss through holes in legs and arms. Securely tie knot so it will not come untied during play. Place arms and legs on back piece aligning holes. Place floss between rectangles of clay on back piece that serve as a tunnel for floss strands. Place a dot of super glue on top of each rectangle. Carefully place baked front piece on top aligning holes. Allow glue to dry, bonding dress front to small rectangle tunnel.

Place an eye pin through each hole making sure pin travels through dress front, arm or leg and dress back. Cut ends of pins to ¼" and curl to secure with round-nose pliers. On front, bend eyes flat against dress. Holding all strings at bottom of jumping jack, test arm and leg movement by pulling down on strings. If movement is fluid, tie strings together in a large knot at bottom. Add a bead to cover knot. Glue clay buttons, cane slices, or ribbon to cover eyes on front of dress. Add additional accessories as desired. Tie ribbon through eye pin in head. Hold pin when making jumping jack move or use eye to hang doll.

Jumping Jack Instructions

MATERIALS: Sculpey miniature face flexible mold • 8 pack of Sculpey Super Flex clay • Liquid Sculpey • 2" eye pins • Embroidery floss • Embellishments • Sculpey blade or craft knife • Pasta machine • Needle tool • Round-nose pliers • Wire cutters • Wood skewer • Acrylic paints • Gel pens • Super glue

INSTRUCTIONS: Condition clay. This clay stays bendable and flexible after baking and is great for toys. With pasta machine set at #1, roll out a sheet of clay for dress. Cut out dress front and back. Carefully use needle tool to make holes indicated on pattern. Cut 4 small rectangles and use a dab of Liquid Sculpey to apply rectangles to back of dress. See photo on page 13 for

Jumping Jacks

Ladies from 1 to 100 will love these articulated creations. Dress them to fit an occasion, a profession or a specific personality… what a treasure!

Dancing Lady

MATERIALS: Sculpey Super Flex clay (Beige, Green, Red, White) • Pink and Green flower and Green and Yellow clay canes • Pink embroidery floss • 12" of 2½" White sparkle ruffled trim • Blonde curly doll hair • Fabri-Tac

INSTRUCTIONS: Mix Red and White to make Pink and Green and White to make Mint. Make bead with Pink and Mint clay. Make jumping jack and head. Cut blouse from Mint and tights from Pink rolled at #1 setting. Form Mint socks around feet and make details with needle tool. Reduce canes to desired size. Cut thin slices of both canes. Pinch Green and Yellow cane to make leaves. Press leaves and slices on blouse and slices on socks as shown. Bake. Glue hair on head with Fabri-Tac and tie ponytail with Pink floss. Glue trim around waist and turn top ruffle down. Tie Green ribbon around neck.

Calypso Lady

MATERIALS: Super Flex clay (Beige, Black, Orange, Red, Yellow, Green) • Premo clay (Burnt Umber, Black,) • Orange and Green flower cane • Orange embroidery floss • Skewer

INSTRUCTIONS: Make bead with Orange, Yellow and Green clay. Mix Beige and Burnt Umber clay and mold head, arms, legs and feet. Make thin Orange logs and twist around arms for bracelets. Blend Orange and Red, roll at #1 setting and cut out dress front. Reduce flower cane to desired size and cut thin slices. Press on front piece for skirt, collar and sleeves. Do not cover holes. Twist thin logs of Orange and Red together to make belt, press on waist. Make jumping jack. For hair roll a thin Black log, wrap around a skewer. Carefully slide off skewer and arrange around face. Attach curls by running thin beads of Liquid Sculpey between curls and face. Blend 3 colors of clay together and cut 2 narrow triangles. Place on sides of head and twist in center. Press a cane slice over twist. Roll tiny earrings and bond to ears with Liquid Sculpey. Bake.

1. Cut the front and back of dress from a sheet of clay.

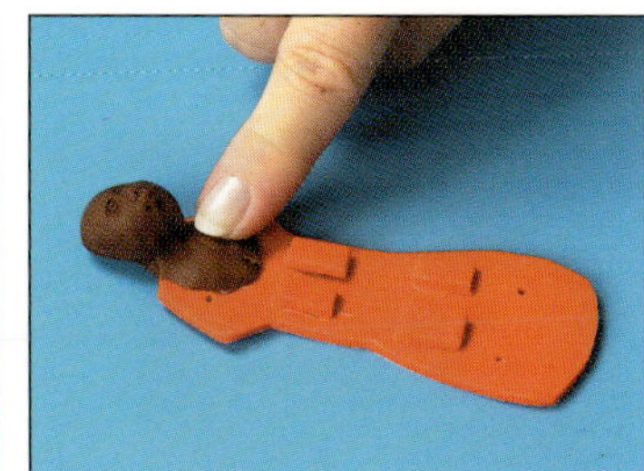

2. Bond the head to the back of the dress.

3. Insert leg in slit of foot and smooth ankle.

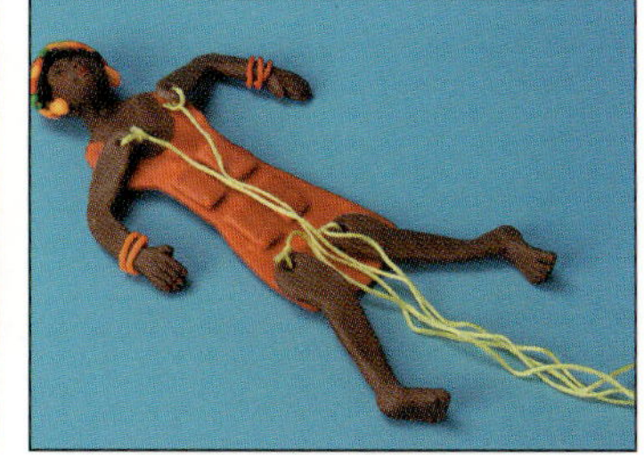

4. Place arms and legs on the back dress piece, align holes and bring thread down.

5. Place the front on back and align holes.

6. Insert eye pin through holes from front to back.

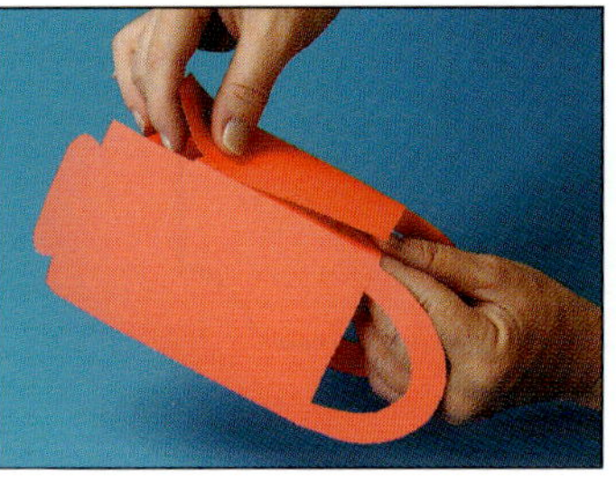

1. Cut slit in back of the bag. **2.** Fold bag and glue sides. **3.** Insert bottom tab in slit.

Gift Bag Instructions

MATERIALS: Sculpey character faces flexible mold • Premo clay • Medium weight tag board • Fabri-Tac
INSTRUCTIONS: Select a theme and a face mold. Mold the face following instructions. Use paints, gel pens or chalks to give your character face a personality to match the gift bag theme.

Trace gift bag pattern on tag board. Cut out bag and fold on dotted lines. Make slit to insert tab. Hold bag in folded position to get an idea of how much decorating you need to do. Glue face on bag. Choose rubber stamps, colored pencils, gel pens, markers, fabrics, buttons, glitter or colored papers to decorate bag. Assemble bag.

Halloween Bag

MATERIALS: Sculpey miniature faces flexible mold • Premo clay (Orange, Green, Raw Sienna, Zinc Yellow, White) • 'Happy Halloween' rubber stamp • Black ink pad • Orange and Yellow gel pens • Black and White paper shreds • Needle tool • Gel pens • White glue
INSTRUCTIONS: Mold Orange faces. Make Green leaves and Brown stems. Press on heads and add details with needle tool. Make very thin sheets of Zinc Yellow, Orange and White. Cut thin strips and press together. Cut out candy corn. Bake heads and candy corn. Add character to faces with gel pens. Cut out bag. Stamp message on bag and color border with gel pens. Glue heads and candy corn in place. Assemble bag. Insert shreds.

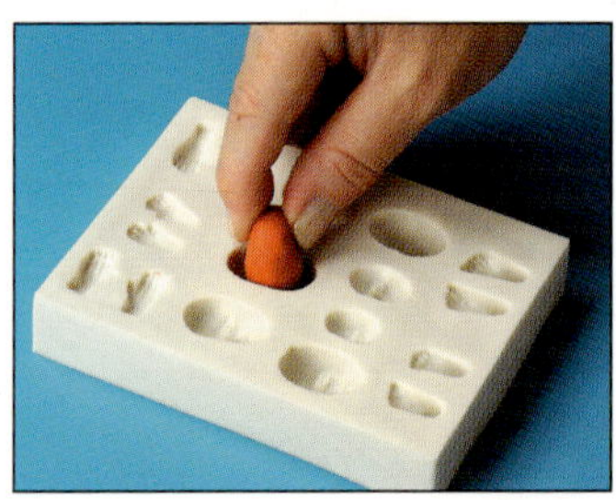

1. Press clay into face mold.

2. Make lines in the face with a needle tool.

Happy Birthday

MATERIALS: Finished doll face • Pink tag paper • White cardstock • White tissue paper • Birthday rubber stamps • Blue ink pad • Colored pencils • Black curly doll hair • 18" of 1/8" Pink wired ribbon • Sticky dots
INSTRUCTIONS: Cut out bag. Stamp birthday designs on cardstock and color with pencils. Cut out. Glue hair on head. Tie bow in center of ribbon and curl ends. Glue doll on bag and ribbon around head. Attach stamped designs with sticky dots. Assemble the bag and insert tissue.

A Special Teacher

MATERIALS: Finished doll face • Scrap of Red clay • Apple clay cutter • Red tag paper • School print paper • Green tissue paper • White curly doll hair • 36" of 1/4" Black satin ribbon • Gold wire • Round-nose pliers • Decorative scissors • White glue
INSTRUCTIONS: Cut out bag. Trim print paper with decorative scissors and glue on front. Cut apples from very thin clay and bake. Make glasses, wrap around face and glue. Glue hair on head and head on bag. Tie bow using 8" of ribbon, glue under chin. Assemble bag. Insert tissue and tie remaining ribbon on handle.

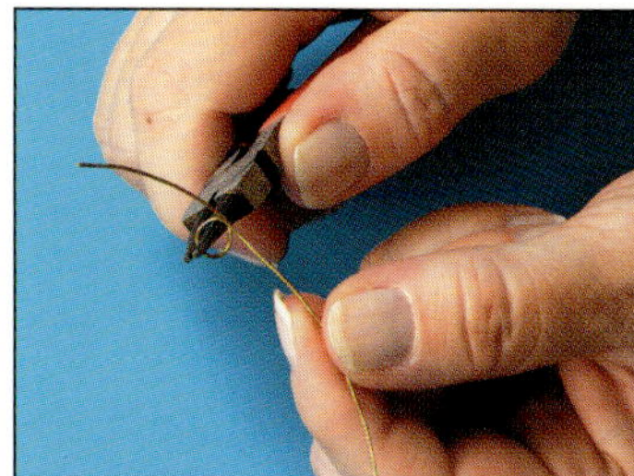

1. Bend a small loop in wire.

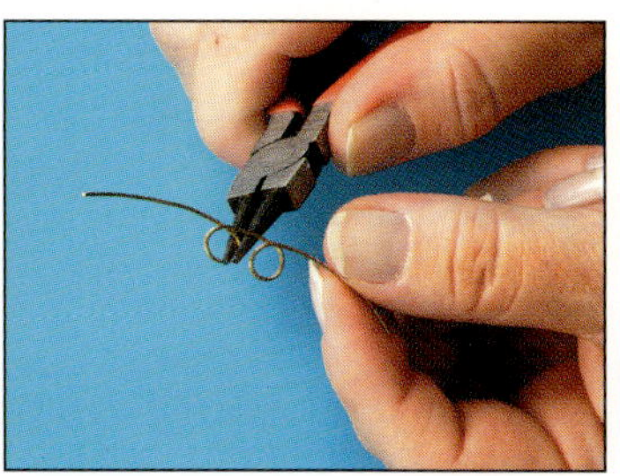

2. Bend a second loop to complete glasses.

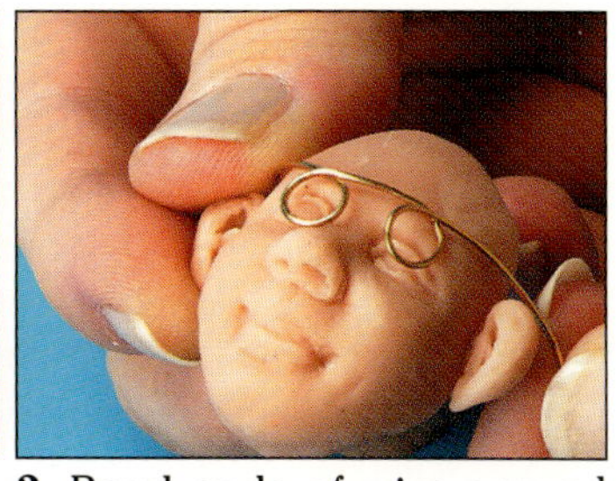

3. Bend ends of wire around the face.

Great Gift Bags

Make these great character gift bags that are decorated with terrific clay doll faces. They are as special as the gifts they contain. Make one for everyone on your gift list. Just change the embellishments to coordinate with the particular occasion!

Happy Birthday Friend!

MATERIALS: Sculpey miniature faces flexible push mold • Block of Beige Premo clay • Two colors of curly doll hair • 1" of Pink fringe • 6" square of Pink tulle • 8" of ⅛" Pink ribbon • 4¼" x 5½" computer printed card or blank card and rubber stamps • Fabri-Tac • Sticky dots

INSTRUCTIONS: Following instructions, mold 2 faces and one set of hands. Open one mouth slightly. Before baking, arrange hands so right hand is on top of left as if friends are holding hands. Bake hands and faces. Paint faces.

Choose a computer generated birthday card background and border. If a computer is not available, use rubber stamps to create the background. Print or stamp birthday message on separate sheet of paper and cut to fit card. Attach to card with sticky dots. Using Fabri-Tac, attach hair to faces. Glue faces on card with hands resting between friends. Glue fringe under one face. Tie knot in tulle and glue under other face. Tie ribbon bow and glue on one head. Write greeting inside.

Grandma & Grandpa

MATERIALS: Sculpey grandma/grandpa flexible push mold • Premo clay (block of Beige, ½ block of Christmas Red) • 3¾" x 8½" Red blank card • 'Grow old along…' and flower rubber stamps • Embossing ink pad • Gold embossing powder • Gray and White curly doll hair • 18" of ½" Gold ribbon • 6" of ⅛" Gold ribbon • Fabri-Tac • Heat gun

INSTRUCTIONS: Stamp words on front on card and emboss with Gold powder and heat gun. Follow instructions for molding face, adding ears and bringing the face to life. Glue hair on heads with Fabri-Tac. Glue faces on card. Cut 4" of ½" Gold ribbon, tie knot in center and glue under man's face. Tie bow with remaining ½" ribbon and glue at top of card. Tie bow with ⅛" ribbon and glue under woman's face. Write greeting on inside.

Santa Greeting

MATERIALS: Sculpey grandma/grandpa flexible push mold • Premo clay (block of Beige, block of Silver, ½ block of Christmas Red) • 5" x 7" White blank card • Rubber stamps ('Merry Christmas', holly, ½" square) • Black ink pad • Red and Green watercolor pens • White curly doll hair • 8" of Gold wire • 6" of ⅛" Green ribbon • 2" square of Red felt • White felt • ½" White pompom • Fabri-Tac • Round-nose pliers • Gel pens

INSTRUCTIONS: Stamp Red and Green holly on card. Roll out a 2" x 5" piece of Silver clay. Stamp with Red squares to look like bricks. Roll and cut out ¼" x 5¼" strip of Silver for chimney edge. Roll out 2" x 3" piece of Christmas Red and stamp Black Merry Christmas.

Push balls of Beige into face #1 and hands. Place mold in freezer for 90 seconds then pop out pieces. Bake clay pieces at 275°F for 30 minutes. Position pieces on card and glue with Fabri-Tac. Color face with gel pens. Glue message, chimney and head on card.

Twist Gold wire with round-nose pliers to form glasses. Glue glasses to top of ears with Fabri-Tac. Add hair for beard and mustache. Cut felt triangle for hat and glue pompom on tip. Glue hat on head and card. Cut ½" strip of White felt. Glue pieces of strip across front of hat and around wrists. Glue hands in place. Tie ribbon bow and glue on message. Write a greeting inside.

Cut-outs Cards

MATERIALS: Sculpey miniature faces flexible push mold • Block of Beige Premo clay • 4" x 5" White blank cards • White paper • Scraps of Blue and Pink paper • *Diamond* rubber stamps showing people at play • Small flower rubber stamp • Embossing ink pad • Red embossing powder • Multi color ink pad • Ink pads (Black, Blue) • Colored pencils • Assorted curly doll hair • 12" of ¼" Red ribbon • Heat gun • Fabri-Tac • Sticky dots • Decorative scissors • White glue

INSTRUCTIONS: Follow instructions for molding faces, adding ears and bringing faces to life. Glue hair on heads. Tie ribbon around one woman's hair. Glue heads on cards. Stamp Blue flowers on upper corners of one card. Stamp Black people images on White paper and color with pencils. Cut out images and attach to cards with sticky dots. Stamp one message on Blue paper with embossing ink. Sprinkle with powder and emboss with heat gun. Stamp other message with multi color ink pad. Attach messages to cards with sticky dots. Write greetings inside cards.

Any Occasion Cards

Need an unusual greeting card for a unique individual? Adapt one of our ideas to fit your specific needs.

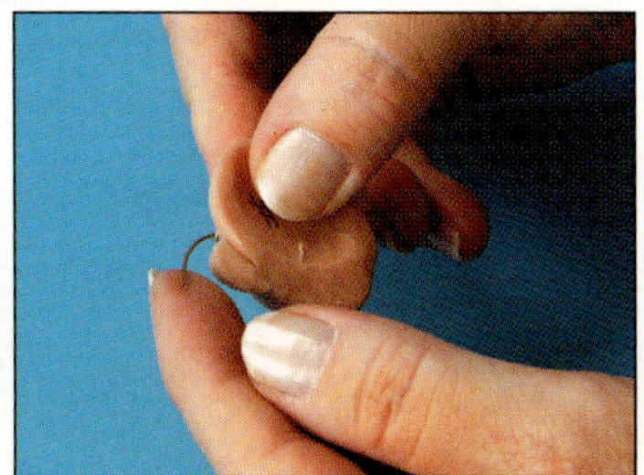

1. Rubber stamp holly on the card referring to photo.

2. Glue ends of the glasses on the head.

3. Glue the bricks on the front of the card.

4. Glue the hat and remaining pieces in place.

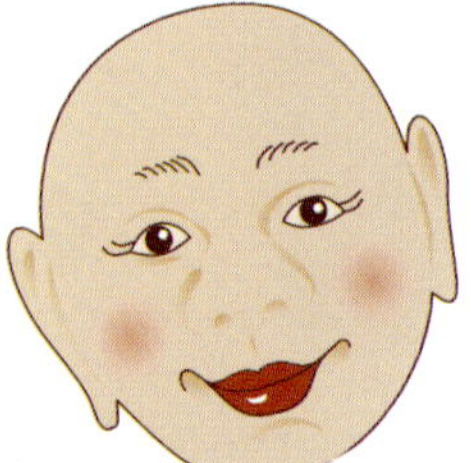

Santa's Snuggly Little Elf

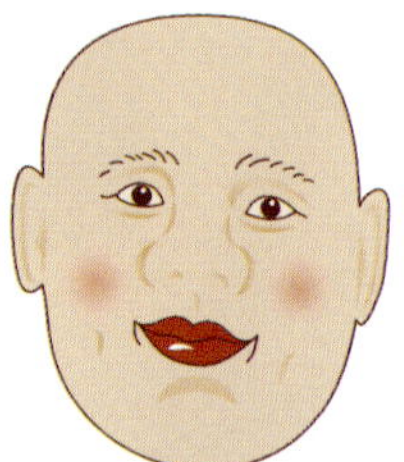

Dark Haired Angel

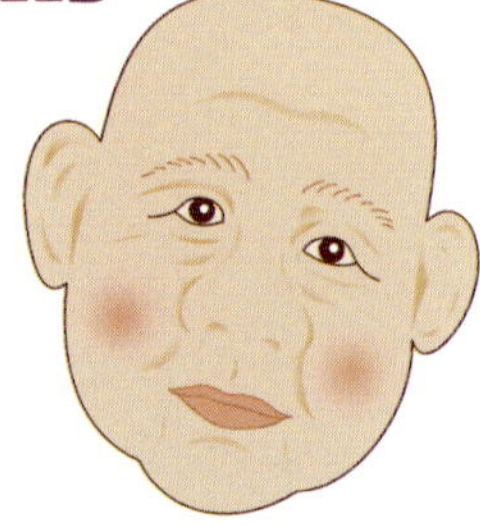

Red Bearded Leprechaun

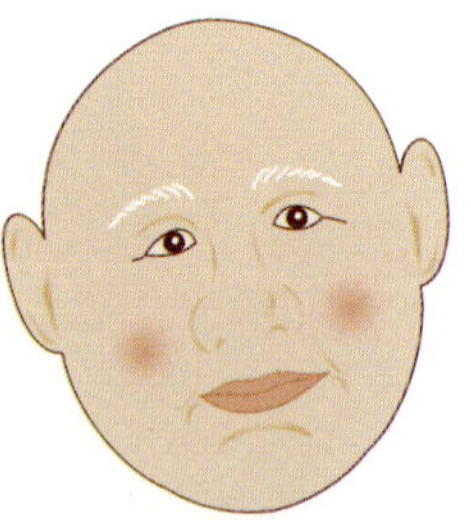

Jolly Santa Claus

YoYo Dressed Scarecrow

Bundled Up Snowman

Lapel Pin Instructions

MATERIALS: Sculpey face flexible push molds • Beige Premo clay • Scraps of colored clay • Decorative paper and scissors • Rubber stamps • Pigment inks • Embossing powders • 1" pin backs • Assorted colors of curly doll hair and nubby White yarn • Miniature hats and scarf • Pompoms • Fabric scraps • Wire • 8" pieces of ribbon or lace • Mini angel wings • Raffia • Acrylic paint • Gel pens • Heat gun • Acrylic sealer • Fabri-Tac • Super glue

INSTRUCTIONS: Follow instructions for molding faces, adding ears and bringing the face to life with paint and pens. Spray the faces with acrylic sealer.

Cut fabric circle and run a gathering stitch around edge. Pull thread tight to form a yoyo. Glue a yoyo under neck of leprechaun, snowman and scarecrow.

For the snowman, tie ribbon bow and glue on yoyo. Glue knitted hat on head and pompon on tip of hat.

For the leprechaun, glue doll hair beard.